I Still Love You

A journey to inner peace...

NERISSA MARIE

This book is a work of fiction; names, characters, and incidents are either products of the author's imagination or are used fictitiously. Any resemblance to actual events or persons, living or dead, is entirely coincidental.

Title Imprint Poetry Books
An imprint of The Quantum Centre, Australia
Published by Happiness Bliss Press
An imprint of The Quantum Centre, Australia

ISBN: 978-1-925647-64-8

Most Happiness Bliss Press books are available at special quantity discounts for bulk purchase for sales promotions, premiums, fund-raising, and educational needs. For details contact books@happinessbliss.com

National Library of Australia Cataloguing-in-Publication entry
Creator: Marie, Nerissa, author.
Title: Poetry Book - I Still Love You (Inspirational Love Poems on Life, Poetry Books, Spiritual Poems, Poetry Books, Love Poems, Poetry Books, Inspirational Poems, Poetry Books, Love Poems, Poetry Books) / Nerissa Marie.
ISBN: 9781925647648 (paperback)
Subjects: Australian poetry.
Australian poetry -- 21st century.

FIRST EDITION

Everyone is in the right place.
Everyone is where they are meant to be in the universe.
~ Robert Adams

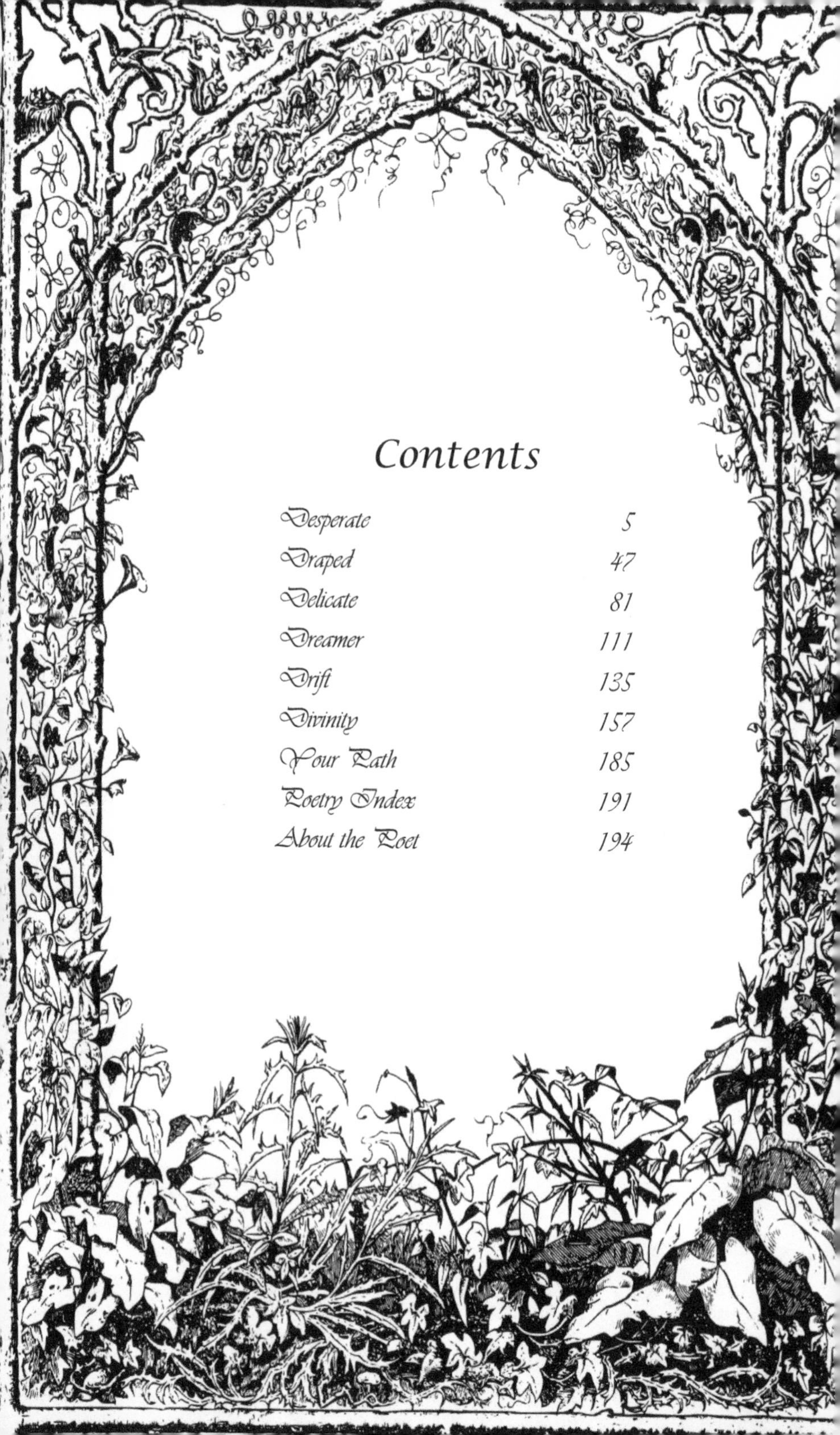

Contents

Desperate

~ Longing. Wanting.

I want *that* to run my life
not my head
not my fears
not the darkness whispering in my ear
That immortal light
That breath of grace
Loves winds tender embrace
The one in charge of villagers plights
The one who causes all the fights
The one who grants life
The first beat of your heart
The breath of eternities promise
The one who started the fire
the pleasure
the pain
In your grace I seek to gain the dissolving of me,
the one floating on mists of duality
Lost in a mirror, crying a river,
surrendering fear
Whilst *you* are always here

For You

Suspended in the air,
you sit and sparkle there
and I just sit and stare
Your gravitational pull, keeps my heart full
Though your light shines down upon me
Though I long to touch thee
I know you no longer love me
So I must embrace natures cruel fate,
to watch you glitter, whilst I wither
Fading in the shadows
My heart has broken
Your name is now unspoken
But when darkness creeps upon me at night,
it's then I search for you in light
and the piece of love you gave me
is the piece that has saved me
For I know that although haunted
I am no longer daunted
by the shadows of wanting to reach out and touch
knowing I loved you too much
For now, you are a simple star,
your love rebounds upon me from afar
and though I see your light
I embrace everything in sight
Each crevice of the universe has created the patchwork of me
this is a love that knows no bounds
and has forever, let me set you free

I Still Love You

Sometimes I think I am a hollow shell
laying on the shore
Waiting for someone to pick me up
and hear the ocean roar

You are a puppet walking on water
balancing until the ocean opens its icy depths
and swallows you whole
There is nothing I can do but watch your fate unfold
This is your destiny,
the only person I can mess with is me
and to you I've already screwed that up
so my advice I'm sure you'd want to chuck
At least I'm free in my pain
with only spirits hope left to gain
I know what they think of me
and that you'd rather avoid this destiny
But I would rather be doused in hate
than ignore loves fate
The beast below flashes as you walk this dangerous path,
one that strips your soul apart
You are not wet,
not one salty drop caresses your breast
Free from sweat, you dance upon the precipice
Salt cleanses
Salt releases
It's sad to watch you try
but I know pity is a lie
I feel the weight of their anchors;
expectation
domination
poisoning your body like radiation
So scared to drown
you entertain all like a clown
Balancing on a tightrope
addicted to the vain hope
that *they* love you

This rope has become your noose
You don't even struggle to get loose
So caught in their trap
No turning back
Unless you throw it all away
then your soul shall be free to sail stray
Billowing winds from heaven above,
shall drive you forwards
Set free with unconditional love

Swallowed

Some say you feel too deep
and from this only sorrow you'll reap
When you are rejected, you lay dejected
When you are hurt, your soul shatters
When you hunger for love,
you sit in the bleak stillness of everything
When a stranger dies, you eject a strangled cry
When you see the beggar on the street,
silent tears greet their feet
But when you love...
the heavens open their doors
and shower the world with songs of eternities grace
The birds sing as your light fluffs their feathers
Rainbows become the forecasted weather
Peace is bestowed upon the world
For your heart is the most sacred pearl

The Gift of You

I am paralysed like a livewire
strung between two posts,
desperate to start a fire,
wanting you the most
Sprinkle water on me, feel my electricity
you'd die from the shock
thus I've remained still as a rock
suspended
un-mended
sparkling with power
Concealed in black, wanting my light back
Travelling through the dark looking for you
Instead I found this light, sparkling in mid-flight

Restricted

In faith between the chapels walls
I lit the candle
Its yellow glow spoke of trust
The martyr gave me faith, to place my hands in yours
To trust that you heard my suffering
That you believed in the betrayal I endured
I did it for you
I trusted in you
I lied for you
I threw my soul to the floor
I maintained I had no worth at all
I followed your scripture, your indoctrinated picture
Because I thought you believed in me, saw the light I could be
So I put up with his slander, his abuse,
the way he tortured my soul
Telling myself you understood
I believed my only hope was to act as you said I should
But now I'm hanging with wounds in my hands
still hoping
wishing
that you would understand
You used my commitment,
and stabbed me through the heart

Sacred Pain

My heart is a cocoon
When I rest in your light,
I open my wings in sparkling flight
Then I get distracted, my focus shifts
and my wings are no longer luminous
From the stars I fall,
tumble
crumble
Till I seek refuge in my heart once more
Here I take shelter in my cocoon
till wings of love fly me beyond the moon
back into the heart of you

Sweetness

My heart is torn, you ripped it in two
and I always thought it was from me loving you
Living in regret I dwelled in the sorrow of abandonment
Stepping out of my body, pretending to be somebody
smarter
prettier
a high achiever
My goals were never reached and it's only me I deceived
feeling, believing, I was unworthy
I came home, back to my heart,
to realise it had never fallen apart
In stillness it speaks
It's always loved me
I just forgot
walking into the swell of life
forgetting my body before birth,
the heart of fire,
why I exist
the place I come from that I so deeply miss

Opened

When you were young
he told you he'd die if you left him
When you were young
he told you he'd always love you
When you were young
he told you if you gained weight he'd buy you a gym,
and lock you in
He couldn't handle you
He told you to laugh when he bullied others
He couldn't handle you
He talked of bombing the enemy
You said you believed in peace
He couldn't handle you
He told you to stop being so opinionated
He couldn't handle you
He told you to be someone different...
tighter, more restrained, more ingrained in the mob
He couldn't handle you
and you became afraid you couldn't handle yourself
But like a wildfire you aren't in control
you are totally out of it
You are
a woman
a dreamer
a fire starter
a wild cannon
a magical mystic
a spiritual warrior
a mistake maker and taker
a being who honours the light of her soul
And I wouldn't have it any other way

Remembering

I swallow
Goodbye. Au revoir.
You travelled so far and didn't want to see me
It upsets me the most that I needed you to complete me
I lay broken ready for death
and you did not sit and watch my illuminated breath
I know you're fake and as I start to reawake
I'll take a new path, escape your farce
and if you every come running
I'll already be gone like dew at dawn
Melting into the ether
forgetting you
forgetting me too
discovering
uncovering
a consciousness that breathes through my soul
Like autumn leaves that fall away to nourish the earth
I experience spirits rebirth
Feeling my heart swell
everything is okay,
all is well

Forgotten

I want to live in an empty cup
so all that's left is for spirit to fill me up
Tearing through my soul
So I can dissolve into the abyss, luminescent mist,
tasting divinities kiss

Sometimes I hate you so
I want to let you go
But I keep coming back, fighting the need to react
I think of the ones who suffer
refugees, bombs killing innocent babies,
using their pain as a buffer
But my heart is linked to you and it will not do
I can't sit in another's misery and expect it to make me calm
So I must claim my pain
watch it sitting there
watch it melt
watch it breathe
I try to reverse time and become a better version,
but at self-worth I am a virgin
So whilst you abuse me, I shall pretend my pain is a lie
one I made up because I feel so yuck
Then I think maybe, I can accept my self-disgust,
the tear, torn across my soul
You never knew me well
and although hate for you in lingers in my psyche
I know to transcend my self-distrust
I must experience peace consciousness
So I simply watch the blown up image of my failure
You've shaken me to the point that to heal
I must begin with the heart of my being
So to spirit I sail my ship
with the pirate flag waving in the sky
I say my final
desperate
goodbye

Succumbing

I see that girl as me lost at sea,
wanting to be, something prettier that she
The internal struggle bruises, your heart is the one who loses
Until we become buoyant, floating along
realising we were never detached from spirits song
Humanities pull is strong
We get caught in the mass sway,
restricting our natural pathway
Unwilling to accept, only open to reject,
the parts of ourselves that are broken
Burying our shame through words unspoken
We landed here and now we want to go back
but it's too late for that
Hand your issues over to life's driving force,
infinite spirit, source
All our desires will melt in the fire
when life picks us up
and we drive to infinite spires

Fragility

The night was dark,
no moon, no glow to illuminate impending doom
I dug deep, cutting black dirt,
inner horrors and self-worth
With shame I look upon the limp shadow
my silhouette, my regret
Death hangs on windless air
capturing secrets with its unending stare
Then I took my pride,
my self-esteem
my visions
my dreams
I buried them so no one would ever see
the bright star I did once hope to be

Surfacing

The time machine has shattered everything that mattered
My hopes lay strung, on experiences that never begun
I am too young to escape the grave
so I sit still and try to behave
I believe nothing I've been taught and yet we unit paralysed,
living lies
Pretending shadows do not haunt
Failures taunt
I am empty to the bone
There is no way I can fit,
the pieces of the puzzle that have fallen away
I fear humanities oppression
What is so wrong that we must escape the eternal chase?
Outsiders seeking identity in this place
Peace is only found in giving up,
in grace

Rugged

I wish the first time I felt your darkness
I ran
I wish when you made me feel like nothing
I ran
I wish when my heart failed to beat
I ran
It rained your empty words upon my soul
It poured your taunts upon my heart
It thundered your abuse
When lightning struck
I ran
Escaping in a dream
Paralysed by your lies, wishing for your demise
If I don't escape now you'll swallow my soul
RUN
'Child of the moon what they say is not true,
for it is love that has made you'
RUN
'Escape the particles of temper that tickle your skin
The violence that lingers'
RUN
Your words are the bridges of cruelty crushed
We all bow to your deception but now I see my own reflection
The hate you hang me with affects me as I let it live
No more shall I play like a fish darting beneath the waves
I see your hook
I shall not reciprocate, eat your bait
It's too late
Walk away
Find another game to play
I shall not bite, not fight
I sit in the nothingness

My vessel is empty because of you
I shall refill my cup with holy water
Of Love, I am the truest daughter

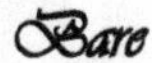

Guilt is like milk dripping in the larder
You try to clean whilst the milk drips faster and faster
Like a soul escaped from the vessel guilt spreads wide
Milk seeps across the bench, white yet penetrable
Still the mess is easy to clean
We want to swallow but are left feeling hollow
Love is the only thing that can purify guilt
removing it with the fluidity of spilt milk

Tainted

I tried to fight you
I'm done
I tried to unite you
I'm done
I feel like my organs are scattered over the floor,
and I am trying to shove them back into my handbag
You are knocking at my door
I'm drained
I'm weak
I'm empty
I'm done
A new journey has now begun

Walking Away

You blew me apart,
put a bullet through my heart
Left me for dead
trapped in the head
I wanted so desperately to please
Feeding the need to succeed
What is life?
If we all await the jaws of death
why do we not count every breath?
Who exists?
Who persists?
Who am I?
Senses are the illusions defenders
They've done well
look around everyone is under their spell
We want to be healers
Yet we no longer understand the source of our beingness
Asking to wake commands the pain of a million lifetimes to
shake our core,
forget all
question your source
Surrender all pain to life's divine force

Shattered

Sometimes I feel like a wall ready to crumble
to fall from the skies and tumble
and I feel your eyes watching me full of curiosity
If I build myself higher, to infinite spires
it'll be a rocky foundation
One that is prone to deterioration
So I don't mind being
hollow, broken, empty
From here I can feel what has made me
The base between my feet
The eyes of God I meet
I know as I embrace eternal wealth,
you wonder if you act with stealth,
Could you remerge in my life?
When everything is feeling fresh and nice?
It's like you're watching a panther
one who's worn and haggard
But your soul is jagged
it wants to run from the one who's begun
the journey inwards
given up all
feeling the loss of their being
wondering if it's God they're seeing
or illusion floating on the dust of confusion
But if I remerge
you will pretend you cared when I faced the knife
internal strife
Through unity I'll see you
But I will not need you
So I shall let you sink back into the folds
as God takes hold

Preserve

Escaping our thoughts is our biggest desire
'I am bad', sucks away our power
We search for emptiness
We try to fill the void of failure with, 'I am good'
Beliefs create nightmares
Sand turns to dirt, as we lower our self-worth
Slip into the void where no thought lingers
Become the bliss you miss
'I am bliss', is a truer thought
But until our mind becomes hollow,
dark and light thoughts will always follow
So watch your thoughts, don't play into the pain,
just watch and true power you will gain
You stand to lose everything,
but from nothing you came

Delusional

Programmed from birth we adventure to Earth,
channels cut,
expectations a must
Succeed,
when it's easier to breathe
Achieve,
when it's easier to just be
Need,
when everything is already free
Locked in school
playing into the hands of those who need our bodies as tools,
machines
I want to scream but my voice is lost
I have hidden my heart in a layer of frost
From this dream we must rise, look beyond the skies
to the reality that lives within thee,
constrained by an entrapped destiny
Until peace rules, we are a race of fools

Looking for Something

Doused in flames dreading the hearts pain
Desperate to live in the shadows of those who reign
My chest is ripped open
broken
breaking
My heart,
scattered
shattered
It feels like everything matters
In self-disgust I reek, seeking approval, fearing disapproval
Dormant emotions wake as my heart surfaces,
floating like a boy on waves
Who am I?
It's all come up, I vomit this muck
past life conditioning, everything is shifting
It's your God take it, I can't fake it
Through cold mud I wade
till the floor turns to glitter, soft beneath the feet
The way to bliss is laden with purity and peace,
dirt and grease
Illusion begins to disappear
Refusing to react I surpass destiny
Spirit is all that's left for me

Sustained

My heart has been cracked open and yet I feel frozen
Poised at the top of a rollercoaster afraid of the drop
Time inches me closer to the rabbit hole
I stay perched not wanting to lurch,
suspended in time
waiting for a push
I jump without a sound, without a whoosh
ready to lose part of my soul
As pieces of me shatter it feels like nothing matters
To you I was just a pawn, something to rub your ego on
I'm letting go, diving off the edge,
this may drive a wedge between us
but I've already seen us,
particles of dust,
thinking to comply is a must
My heart, soul, body and breath
come undone

Loosening

We are water and some of us drown
lost at sea, till we merge with thee
Thinking we are the drop when the world is an ocean
We individuate till we merge into the body of love
Water that rains from heavens above
We are the storm,
the thunder pour,
dew drops at dawn
nothing more, nothing less
Undress the parts you thought were separate
Your desperate nakedness
Your body is sacredness,
a miracle of liquid
Feel the presence of you as you merge, re-emerge
with *that*
that bliss,
that grace
You belong in this sacred place

Perceived

When life feels like a series of fault lines
and your breath is so shaky you feel you can only gasp
walking through life wearing a fear mask
You're ready to crack but we don't want that
For if you fall apart the Earth will crumble
and into its molten depths we'll all stumble
Those who want to break you
are not the singular force that made you
Falling into darkened gaps you let them whip your back
Like a horse and cart you plunder on
pretending nothing is wrong
and all you want is to run away
The magic of life is hidden in vaults
leaving you to think
abundance is found by tapping into another's wealth
Healing, happiness, is the breath of you
of which you are a piece of too
Claim your divine power
Do not cower
For the ones who make you feel meek
it's your light energy they seek
You are made of spirits eternal glow
All who would take this from you
have fallen into fear, forgetting love is ever near
Like the horse you buck, down on your luck
Until you unfold from the mental glue that controls you
Slip into the stream
Embrace the dream
Don't fear the scream
Be breath
Disconnect
Resurrect yourself as a beacon of light

One who has not lost sight
Escape the pain
Pull out of the game
Reclaim the divine right to be you
For you are divine and worthy of spirit too

Your Strength

We are scared to breathe,
speak
participate
take risks
and yet we were born to die
We paint our faces, dress in silks, perfect our bodies
Hiding under skin, forgetting we never did begin
Upset with ourselves for the ugliness felt
failures, forgetting, regretting,
worrying, suffering, disconnecting
If the body is not real and we are left fighting change,
are we insane?
Who am I?
Is the breath of wisdom
Forget the system
Scents of flowers, internal power
The breath of 'I'
The physical illusion we all seek to deny
You are beyond form
You surpass the norm
What is conscious?
Look to the heart, feel the presence of grace,
the sacred place from which you emerge
A visual perception that cannot be captured in words
You are warmth in the heart, silence of breath
The grace of unity where the soul likes to rest

Transforming

We want to write our pages as though we are reflections
of all the beauty we see in the world
And yet we kill our spirit when we try to write a script
that is out of our control
The arms of death are those that shall forever hold us
and yet we let this world mould us
I wish I could blend with you
your culture
your beliefs
your happiness,
so pure and true
I feel
scared
scarred
Against rough winds I have faired
But when I look behind the glamour of your face
I see a holy light, divine grace
This is the reflection that I want to share in, merge with
But only when I see the divine reflected in my shadow,
shall live a sunny tomorrow

Scripted

Draped

~ Covered so as to render invisible.
Hidden from view.
(But we all know it's there.)

The ego is a tiger, a ravaging beast
Upon your soul it likes to feast
and yet you think it cares for you
whilst it belittles every little thing you do
Your notions,
your intentions
they feed the hungry
whilst you are left starving
for love from the heavens above
Breathe into the pain
Strike the ego
Don't answer its call
In silence you'll discover the truth of your being
It's only illusion you have been seeing
You are no-thing
The space from which you arise
ego arises
Let go
Watch
Surrender
and be consumed by *that*
that nothing, that grace, that sacred place
Beyond everything you've
heard
read
seen
All that's left is infinite bliss,
illuminated nothingness

Casting Light

Your aura is cracked through seeds of pain
repetitive affirmations heard again and again
You start to believe it's true, harsh words spoken by others
Cruel words seem to erupt within you
Pictures in papers reinforce the lashings of the soul takers
Pain and desire chip the shell
the sacred place where the soul likes to dwell
The aura opens to reveal your light
to which the darkness revels in full flight
They start to suck your light energy
the moment your soul begins to swim free
Turn away from fear, from lust,
turn darkness and spells to dust
When you don't react you become impenetrable
Surround yourself with light, everything is alright
You are perfect
You are whole
Rebuild your shell resting in the truth,
all is well

Sacred Shell

You are playing a role,
one where you disown your own soul
So dedicated to the act you instantly react
The perfect performer
The actor has become the character
You think your mistakes are a path you've decided to take
But the script was written for you, before you arrived,
before you began to think that you are alive
and it has overtaken all sense of reason
You've dissolved into the seasons
thinking the circulation of planets is real
that everything is solid because you feel
Wake up from the play
Realise you are not the script
You are the essence of consciousness
Each line you speak is a map, a reflection back
Dissolve the illusion of separation
You are one with creation
You are air before words, between worlds
The story unheard
Like the glitter of stars upon the sea, you are a reflection
Life has obscured your perception
Become the artist of the star painting this world from afar
You are the light
The gaps of empty space
The moon spun by the sun
You are not someone
You are the heart from which you are never apart
A silence that has no words
A play dissolved into the disarray
By love you are bound, through the heart centre found

Transcend

Love is your name
Hate, the knot binding your soul
You believe need to control, that which is you
In desperation you strive to stay alive
unable to surmise breath that is freely given
Unquestioning the touch of your body, your sacred birth,
the journey of life on Earth
So caught in the sweep of expectation
you guide your life's path with fear's domination
Peace is your essence
To heal rejection's lashings surrender to your soul,
the infinite peace residing in you,
the blessing of love living through your mind
The heartbeat of creation that makes you believe you're alive
Reach for compassion
Forgive your soul
Forgive the needy
Forgive desperate beings who are bleeding fear
Knowing that you are love
Grace is the breath of each being,
the reflection of life you are living
Love is your heart beating

Love's Reflection

I hate pain
I hate rape
I hate hate
I hate this mix
I hate that when I look around there's so much I want to fix
I hate the human hood
I hate that I want humanity to act exactly as I think it should
seeing souls instead of pasts
instead of
colour
country
religion
To love I must grasp
I hate this poisonous word is the one that wants to be heard
I want to merge through the mirror of consciousness
To exist in bliss
I watch the thoughts I hate with love

Learning Forgiveness

Depression is a coma,
where one waits for the trauma of life to be over
Sitting at the station, bathed in inner frustration
Waiting for a lift to purity consciousness
Forgetting we are reflections of light living an experience
Humanity is delirious, and the depressed are those waking up
You need to feel the pain, the shame,
your self-worth maimed, to uncover there is only love to gain
You are here as an act of grace
You belong in this sacred place
Pain tells us we are not okay,
this is nature's way of healing, reminding
encouraging the seeker to look for truth behind the mind,
beyond suffering, beyond remembering
Forgive your imaginings
Forgive the illusion of you
Sail forth on this moments wings
Dissolve self-doubt that niggling self-hatred,
you know what I'm talking about,
by watching the suffering
Acknowledge the agony
Holding hands with bliss, forgiveness, presence,
the ever-present joy acceptance brings
You are the peace in all beings

Recognising You

You felt there was no hope left for humanity
Darkness shadows mental clarity
We are hanging to a piece of string
which has withered to a thread
Then light took over the night
I saw the star shooting across houses afar
and I knew it was a sign, to let go of the thread
and fall into the ocean of light, trusting everything is alright
We cling to a reality that is nothing short of insanity
But I believe in you and I know you trust me too
two
us
together
Against evil clouds we sit, enduring stormy weather
Feeling the rains sting, embracing the hope it brings
Knowing what *they* tell us to believe is all a lie
Life is glorious
We will be victorious
as we hold the hands of light and dissolve the night

Charmed

We pride ourselves on being non-materialistic
yet not even a shadow of our life is simplistic
Too caught in the mind are we,
to ever let ourselves just be
just breathe
just see
the nature of spirit
the nature of us
Soon they'll be digging our grave
and we shall still be wondering...
What's the polite way to behave?
We are a nation of slaves born to obey
But it is our ego of which we are most afraid
We burn like cinders at dawn, till once again we are reborn
Melt into the flame where you claim the light within
that makes you remember you never did begin
There is no end in sight
No light to reflect the night
This is our forgotten plight
The reality we are trying to procure is so obscure
it doesn't exist
There is nothing we've missed
We always have been,
always shall be,
divine beings of pure consciousness

Undone

We are all creeps wanting to peep on Instagram
at our friends and enemies' life plan
The next best thing would be to go to their house
take a good look about, see all their stuff
and lament we are not enough
We are nosy like mice not thinking twice
When we search others for all we lack we turn our back,
on innocence
Happiness is found within
not ravaging through someone's life bin
You know you're wasting your time online
It's all a trap
You're putty in their hands, the ones who want you distracted,
unresponsive, non-reactive
Remember to live
Remember to give
Warmth of the heart is where happiness opens its wings

Confined

The demons live inside my head
They attack every time I go to bed
Alive on multiple panes of reality
they try to warp your perception of destiny
Struggling to break free from monotony
the controlling hands of material monopoly
I fear if others could see inside my mind
they'd bound me tight and tell me I'm not quite right
But as my perception shifts
this whole place becomes a silicon sea
slipping in and out of reality
The force is one
The place from which your soul begun
Nothing matters
Illusion shatters
Take a new road, one lined with trees grown in luminous soil

Horizon

I'm scared of this world, this inner turmoil
People are fighting, striking like bolts of lightning
I don't understand God's master plan
Why am I to discover the source of 'I Am'?
The knife is at my throat
I forget every word I wrote listening to another note
air, breath, the seed of bliss
that shall plug me into happiness
nirvana
satcitānanda

Fluid Pain

I am your worst nightmare a rebel beyond proportions
who will never bow to your distortions
I salute the light within
It's loves song that I sing
Watching pain in silence
Reacting with non-violence
Feeling the cords break
Dissolving shackles of hate
Illusion is clear when we surrender fear
Mists are melting
Following the heart
Honouring destruction, the shadow,
creates a meadow of blossoms
A happiness life has forgotten

Blooming Grace

Perfectionism haunts our core
In desperation we fight to be more
more than *that*
more than us
more than grace
We live at the shores of a horror ridden place
Unwilling to face
the darkness
suffering
agony
that lies within
Our vision is blurred, life obscured,
by the idea that we aren't enough
You were created as a gift
a sparkle of luminous consciousness
Rest into your pain
There is only peace to be found
when you let your will slow down
Struggling to create an affirmation
that will dissolve your creation
is fighting a battle with life itself
For one thing I am glad spirit thought to create you
For when I am broken and feeling bent on self-regret
I shall know that another has felt this anguish
Salty wounds surfacing under a full moon
and through their suffering has discovered a wealth unnamed
Peace in spirit, in this moment
Escaping our skin will do nothing
You never did sin

You were created by spirit and where you fail so does God
There never was anything wrong
for God is light and love and so are you
You were made by divinity
You float in infinity
and your soul it just breathes
When you fail to squeeze the pain away
and surrender to the notion that it's here to stay
You become a pillar of strength, empowerment
For in your flaws is hidden the most magnificent truth
that you are an embodiment of light,
to feel loved is your divine right
Our being is warmed as we surrender to the storm
Discovering light is our essence and we are all luminescent

A Hint of Light

Throw the match and watch them burn,
the powers who like to discern
broke from broken
The jigsaw puzzle, trapping your soul in a vicious muzzle
The muscle of minds that like to define the laws of mankind
You are kind
You are kindred
Kindle the inner flame
Escape the rulers who dictate
that you must live enveloped in hate

Light Compassion

The world is the apple tainted with poison
The serpent fed you and now you walk in a living dream,
concussed
asleep
In the Garden of Eden desire you breathe
feeding a need for reality
I'm thinking, I'm thinking
Thought is lust
Reaction creates karma, the fuel of this drama
But who exists and will life persist?
Wake whilst you are alive
Right and wrong makes you think you belong
Words unsaid
Pages unread
Trapped inside my head
Refusal to wake
I'm naught but a piece of glass unwilling to break,
slaving to emotions
As the drug of life dissolves, your heart unfolds
The world doesn't exist, it never did
You don't exist, you never did
Suffering and pain doesn't exist, it never did
You are the screen
Wake up, life is not what it seems
The serpent is temptation
The world, desire itself

We split society by having better schools for those with more jewels

They are scouring the Earth looking for lights,
anyone who appears shiny and bright
It's your courage they want
Your confidence too
Anything that makes you transcend the fears living within you
On social media they possess your person, filtrating the system
injecting fear, shame and guilt
It's your spirit that gets spilt
Pull back
Retract
As they slither along
venom ready to slip into anyone singing a positive song
Own your fears, confessions and doubts
They want you to feel like a layabout
You are made from the fibres of God,
as are your sins, your shortcomings
so embrace them with love
Let your body, soul, and breath be enriched in this moment
All you need is to pull the cord from the dream
realise it's illusion you're seeing
Melt into the chest where the breath is felt
let the hallucinogen melt
Anything you've experienced is a vision,
not a determination of your soul's projection
You are neither good or bad
You are not sad
There is nothing you never had
Feel the love that breathes through you
and realise you are made of this too
There has never been something wrong with you
You are the queen
You are the beggar

You are the sword, the arrow of thought
Retract to the heart
You don't need to react
Escape confusion
Subtract from the illusion
Merge with love

Sparkle

Mind riots, refusal to keep quiet,
the battle is in my head
Many soldiers are wounded, many are dead
There is no time for revoke
It's these thoughts my mind wants to choke
Questioning the source of 'I'
I realise everything is a lie
I'm walking around thinking I'm me when really I'm nobody
I want to fit in, but then my mind wins
Why is it I who wants to question?
Burning for spirits resurrection
Death seeks me, 'I' completes me
With this sword I cut all thought
Who am I?
From where do I arise?
Time on Earth is short,
we remain confused, consumed by thought
I want to melt the source of my illusion
so the hand of spirit is all that's left
Comparison is the minds greatest weapon
I accept my failure
my fears
my demise
and with this surrender
I rule the mind's eye
Making no effort in this resting place
Defeating the mind with eternal grace

Spirits Sword

We are taking names on the astral planes
Do not think the definition of good
is acting as your fellow humans think you should
The herd acts upon righteousness
Those who pillage, who burn humanities village
are being watched
Escape the race
The need to judge by the colour of a face
Innocents incarcerated
Tears shed
Judgements bled
Anger
Hatred
Greed
These are the powers of darkness ignoring our creed
The untouchables are those at the top
floating on money solid as rocks,
making others feel small,
as though they have no worth at all
The way you make others feel means a great deal
When you meet us you will learn lies do not deceive us
Stand tall
Stand strong
Sing your hearts song
Forget who you are supposed to be,
allow your soul to run free
If you knew the power invested in you
you'd know exactly what to do
you'd love yourself for all your flaws
and this would open unseen doors
When your feet leave this place floating into the abyss of grace
you will retrace, the steps you took,

the lives you shook
You've been led to think your bad
to wish for things you never had
Rise
Watch the darks demise
those who blind your self-esteem with lies
Get out of the trap
Take your life back
Transcend existence
Release persistence
You are wide awake
Strength is found in holy grace
You manifest from this sacred place
Take aim
Regain your power
Unfold the holy lotus flower

Lights Prayer

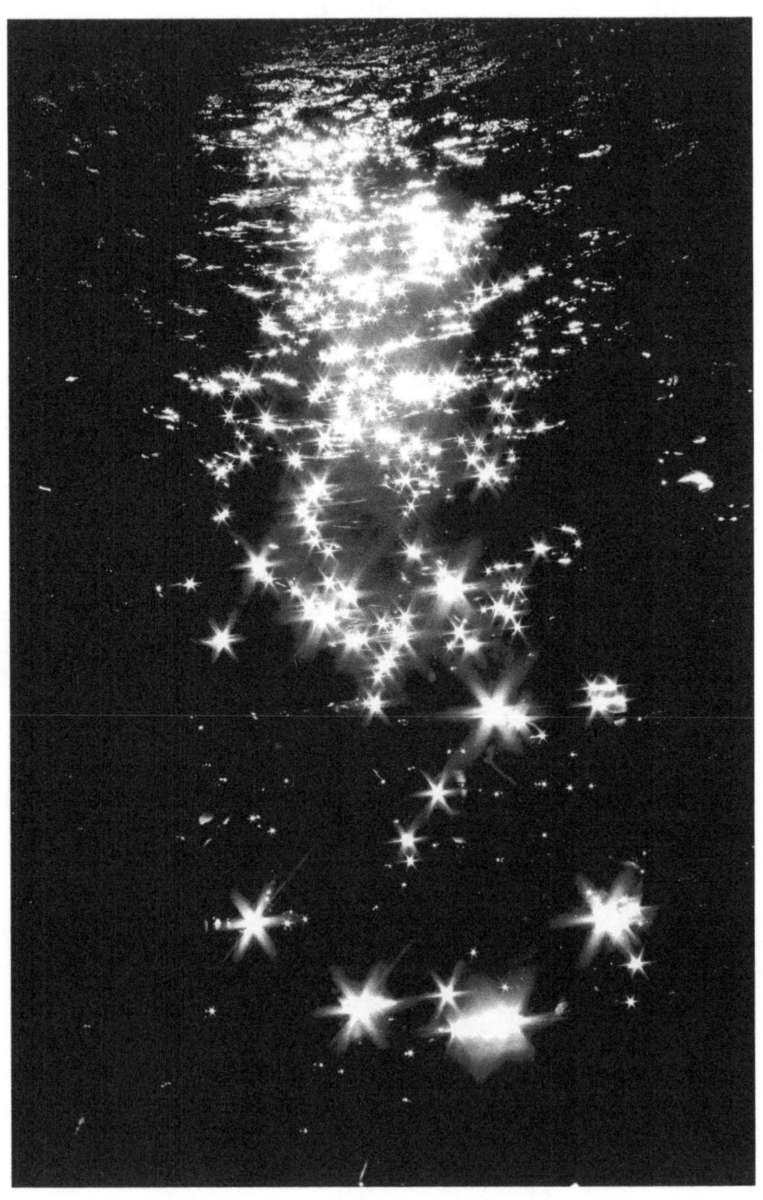

We inject venom under our skin pretending it's medicine

Split between two seas there is no place for me
You hover on dry ground as we wait to watch you drown
I crave the oceans touch
The veins that run from shore to shore
linking us forever more
I reach out then dive back
Escaping consciousness, eluding time
Making everything about me, my and mine
And yet this leaves me feeling hollowed
My heart the ocean has already swallowed
There is no place for me
So I must dive in
Breathe
Start to be
Surrender to the tide, the moons pull, the ocean swell
The place beyond my mind where all is well

Roots

Delicate

~ Handle with care

We live like delicate threads of lace
with not a piece out of place
For a string of red, silhouettes white
We fear bloodshed, burying our emotions
for those we see plant seeds of envy
Walking on water we paste images of our mastery
Displaying our perfections for others
But what lies beneath the sea?
A murky torrent of water
Shame fills our sons and daughters
We feel hollow,
empty volcanoes devoid of liquid strength,
flames of golden innocence
Feel the dirt, the shame, the unworth
You are beautiful in this moment
this breath
this essence
The string of you binds you to others
Let go in love, float above
and into the stillness beyond this life
travel
release
rest
Caress your pain, it's part of you
making it sacred too
There is no difference between stars resting upon the ocean
and life in motion
Feel the whispers of the waves
Float across liquid light
Feel your heart surrender to peace
There is nothing to do
Accept the grace of you

You're reflected in happiness
Let your heart, soul, body and breath, rest

Touched

Regret is the shadow of unworth
Life tinted with suffering
We obsesss over
manifesting
creating
being
When we are already here, present
Find presence in suffering,
presence in pain
Until love is the only desire which does remain

Why We Are Here

We wear our fears like black overcoats
clasped too tightly at the throat
Hoping they shadow us in blackness
so we can drape inside the closet,
hiding amongst others in darkness
Like entities crave the light, we crave black
Covering our back, hoping to distract
the world from our flaws
Seeking rewards in good
But the definition of angelic is predetermined
by men who drone in sermon
We've forgotten our nature
Draped in covers, hiding from one another
avoiding those who sting
Forgetting to treat them as a lover from a failing fling
Bring forth your nakedness
Your bereft sacredness
You are innocence,
majesty,
sacred breath
In spirits heart, rest

Hanging

I don't think God knows I'm here yet
for I cannot feel grace yet
I am still not fearless
I live in the web my mind has spun
Suffocating under the weight of illusion
I fear it would be easier to slip into delusion
I don't measure up
I am tall you see, but I am not free
This world feels tight
longing for laughter and light
I know the darkness is after my disconnection
I escape into inner reflection
Still searching for the mirror,
that will prove spirit is here

Courage

My ego is a seeker, a total pleasure keeper
Everyone tells me to love it
But I just can't seem to rise above it

I placed the pain inside my throat,
a burning scream
One that could not be heard as I am too reserved
to acknowledge my fear,
my past
Admiring others, sinking in shame
Tearing myself to pieces again and again
Is it the poison of sin I'm feeling?
Why must I speak when my soul feels weak
If I see love in all, why am I afraid of the butchers call?
I reach for the stars and fears come to meet me
Many lifetimes dissolve into this experience
We need to hear the voices of the broken
Who else would acknowledge that we long to be fixed?
Transfixed on the precipice of suffering and hope
Let it be
becoming the seed of light growing into the blossoming tree
I seek thee, honour thy soul
When I am too scared to breathe, aghast at the hatred I see
I grow my hands at the base of love
and surrender my bones to the awakened throne

Seed of Light

We want to be recognised
Fighting our egos demise we flounder
as we fail to be less than an all-rounder
Yet to whom do we praise?
And does worship of validation,
sooth the soul of self-imposed degradation
It's not about what others think
as we strive to be recognised in life's rink
Ducking and diving, we hide behind striving
Eluding our soul, the story of us
Forging direction with glamour's lust
Our light is fading, ego breaking,
as we struggle to feel, make everything real
Making our life neat
Thinking we need to compete
Wither
Melt
Illusion is felt as you grasp through swirling darkness,
devoid of oneness
The ego doesn't need recognition
and spirit knows that
It's why we are trapped as we try to achieve,
forgetting to see the humbleness of being
Realising in failure it's only love you are seeing
Accept failure as progress, the gurus test
caresses from destiny
the call of humility
Must we fight to control the way our story unfolds?
The way we are heard?
Light tickling the ears of dreamers
Let yourself just be realising grace can set your heart free
Each breath is a gift surrender to this
Find the hero in air

let your presence rest there
here
now
the light will devour your illusional source of power
Swim in an ocean of presence,
realising light is your essence

Presence

We are afraid of broken pieces
Shards of glass are easily swept,
compared to a mind ingrained in concepts
Until we feel, we poison ourselves with pain
When your heart breaks you return to nothingness once again

Floating in a little boat to a foreign shore
leaving their country where they have a home no more
All so rulers can profit from war
Profit from fear
Profit from the darkness of terror
Upon reaching modern shores people are locked away
The foreign dream never wanted them anyway
Like dogs crowded in rescue shelters they wait for hope
Whilst their hosts blind themselves with propagandas dope
Ignorance is our best distraction
We cannot even see inside where they are kept
Under the carpet the unwanted are swept
Children are molested, women raped
and we respond to the victims with hate
Abandoned hope
Torn shores
Refugees return home with a *you're not welcome note*
Children are blown into little pieces, scattered upon the land,
dissolving into particles of sand
How low will humanity sink?
Stealing breath from those who live on the brink
Their boat has sunk
Ghosts walk upon the ocean bed,
the only place it's safe,
for the unwanted ones to rest their sorry head

We leave high school with no self esteem
ready to live out the Western dream
Lights. Camera. Action
Can I get a reaction?
But the vessel is hollow
struggling to find a path to follow
You may fall asleep,
wake up and not recognise where you are, life has travelled far
Yet you've stayed stagnant
A remnant of misery is all that's left of you and me
So what happened to the dreams?
Why did life become loose at the seams?
A pouch with a hole where everything falls out
You have fallen through the cracks,
unable to get your life back
Take my hand, together we can take the road less travelled
and look for that which we never lost,
allow our hearts to defrost
Possessions are measured in gold and diamonds
Let's take a new road, one where we search
for diamonds in the heart
The school of eternal destiny
There is more strength to be found in not I but we

Unravel in love
Travel in light
Do not identify with the wrongs of the world
You are the tummy
I am the foetus
There is no need for air between us
The world is your cradle
Floating through this experience
The appearance of your life as a mess,
in rags and ruins,
is not truth
It is the 'I' that sees that
Makes you think that you are less than thee
Makes you think you're separate from me
But me isn't a real thing, for I am nothing
You manifest from holiness
There is no truth in separateness
Search for your light

Birthing

Man is so arrogant that his God must look just like him

Where are you going to go when you die?
The minds perception is a lie
You're already in hell when you
judge
begrudge
suppress
follow the rest
No need to regress till the fires swallow you up
You don't deserve to be in hell
just because you're down on your luck
We limit ourselves
burying our hearts in sand as we bow to the man
When foreign ships embark on our planet
they'll think we're insane
Trapped in fear waiting for life to disappear
Hating one another
Addicted to a screen
that tells us who to love and who is supreme
Take a hammer and break the dream

Lucidity

Like candles we burn out, hunting to unite our flame
to start a fire
to melt in heat
to eradicate defeat
Yet the wick burns low, and we are left shallow
devoid of light, slipping into the night
melting into the dream
ripped at the seams
Pools of wax
Bated breath lusting in regret
Remembrance of brightness,
melting into illusion

A refugee floats at sea, sitting in a boat
carried by winds of hope
Praying for love and dry land
open hands
Onwards to kinder shores,
escaping the wrath of bloody wars
I don't know what to say to one who could walk away
from the cries of the suffering
I pity your shame, your hollow pain
May gentle hands caress your back, helping you to not react
Don't let suffering remind us of horrors met with blindness
If they were your family you'd let them be
Greeting with open arms and warm hospitality
May you see you are a child of divinity, breathing through one heart
Love *is where healing starts*

Blinded

Have no worry for where you stand
for you are simply more than woman or man
Do not cling to misfortune
for you enter with nothing and leave without
So what's the virtue behind all these things you worry about?
Let your worries be handled by source
the place you manifest from of course
Compassion is the place from where we heal
Spirits feet, the place to kneel
Forgive and forget
Don't hold onto hate, love or regret
Let everyone go
Let love flow
and you will discover the seed of light in your heart
from which you are never apart

Peace in Presence

I'm scared that I'm here, that everything feels so near
My mind is shadowed in illusion
My skin pale, all light diffused, my brain amused
Yet my heart is caught
warped
trapped
I want reality back
This place is a lie
a planet veiled in disguise
Eyes stare
People care
But we all die
and we think we know why, what, how and when
What happens when this comes to an end?
Crumbles
Falls
Broken
Breaking
I cannot fuse into a tamed soul
Yet I lurk pretending to wilt looking to feel beyond my heart,
to a lost lover's caress
Sworn to exist my ego persists but every piece of me resists
The strain of thought desires nothings reward

Peace in That

You are not the body
Thank God for that
You are not the sum of your experiences
Thank God for that
You are not the taunts of your mind
Thank God for that
You are not your critics review
Thank God for that
Let the world pass through the mind from this you arise
Bring forth your egos demise
with no thought, no effort
You are the nothing from where stars arise,
dragonflies at dawn
Your journey never begun
You are the light behind the sun

Discovery

You are the raindrop falling in fear
wishing you could just disappear
Criticism is the wind that whips
Bitterness settles upon your lips, a salty sting
that makes you feel you are worth nothing
The air is humming, with the taste of your breath
Desiring satisfaction, all you seek is reaction
You are falling,
crying,
calling
You are lost
Your soul covers in frost, an icy hail, at life you've failed
You are anything but nice
Just a cold arrow of ice
A worthless blip, streaming through the abyss
Down you go, plummeting deeper into the ego
You hit the ocean
Your heart is set in motion
As you begin to melt you experience
self-love
compassion
bliss
and you realise you were always this
Like autumn leaves your heart breathes
slipping from the tree
The clouds suck you up and again you fall
till you merge with the ocean
and realise you always have been
one with all

Patterns

You are the grace of the heart found within all beings

Dreamer

~ One who lives with their head in the clouds.

The morning air bites darkness that was never there
We arise as our soul slips into our body
Memories mumble our mind
pushing all thought in an abstract line
We believe we exist
We believe we must persist
We walk and talk till our soul slips away
and we await once more the birth of a new day

Sacred Birth

We're looking for drugs to take us above
to escape this place, dissolve the human race
You're living in maya
Shooting up illusion, high on delusion
Your rights, your fights, are a piece of your imagination
You are the dreamer, addicted to the ego
The drug has taken over
Now you think what you see is real
Trapped, all you do is react
The only way to escape the high is to realise everything is a lie
The world rises with you
All that surrounds is a reflection of light
So be kind to all and press delete on the need to repeat
this dream of creation,
this imagination,
this liquid love
Your mind is a liar that needs to rot
You are the addict
You are the heart
You need nothing
No one
From you the source of creation has begun

Moments of Maya

You arise with the mind as morning is dawning,
and dissolve into night without warning

Let go of everything
Everything is a spell
In the heart truth dwells
All is well

Sometimes we need to trust
even when we think to control everything is a must
You can't erase your past
You can't predict your future
But you can realise you don't exist
and dissolve into bliss
We trap our soul with the need to control but the door is open
You are not broken
Wherever you've been forgive the dream
trust the process,
holiness in breathing,
love is all you are ever receiving
All context of dual, are merely intellectual
You are desiring to escape the simplicity of being
Yet your heart remembers, it's only love you're seeing

Valuable

I feel like the jewel in the crown,
the one that has fallen loose,
dissolving into the eternal spoof
The diamond that has turned to dust
Renounce materialism
Renounce ego
Yet I desire to be loved
I hear the angels above call but I cannot break the wall
of fear, shame, regret
Maybe if I was normal life would make more sense
but I am one of those people laced with crazy essence
A piece in the puzzle that does not fit
I feel my heart starting to slip into the pain of others grief
From suffering is there no relief?
Fall into the bleakness
Discover uniqueness
Hollowness evaporates into the light which radiates
behind the mind
ending all fate

Riches

I'm an optical illusion clouded by confusion
my thoughts are my worst enemy
I poison them with self-inquiry

Thoughts are a painter's splatter, the heart in tatters
The mind believes everything matters
With each question
Who thinks this thought?
A stroke of white removes the tainted colour
Who am I?
A stroke of white removes the tainted colour
Until only the canvas remains

Faith's Palette

Your mind is a bit crazy you see
It manifests everything you see
It's better to let everything just be
Then you will be free

Anger is a toxin that poisons your veins,
permeates your brain,
tinting your perspective borderline insane
If you swallow your anger, you it eat too
and we both know that's no good for you
When anger is fluid like a liquid melody
peace is a simple remedy
It's the anger that lodges that damages your life
Let it charge your body, feel its power explode
from a bud to a rose
Anger is the thorn inviting scorn
keeping you torn from the depths of your essence
your beauty
your luminescence
Stay present
Don't play anger on repeat
Their problem is their pain, delete its sacred song
No one was ever wrong
Like visions they damaged you
But what if there was only one?
The light of the sun
Bow to your pain
Regain,
the light of you
that was clouded in black
Take your immortal power back

Hurts Heart

Live like you are already dead

Do the dead watch us like stars from a reality series?
Do they shudder as we tear our souls?
Struggling through life, chasing mindless goals
Pretending we know it all, that we will never fall
When the guillotine of death heartily awaits us all
So caught up in the sweep are we
it must be easy to laugh at the flaws of our simplicity
Why are we here?
What are we trying to be?
The danger of life is that we think we have it right
Whose programme do we follow?
And are we all stars?
And what really happens, when we wake up to who we are?

Shining

We think we are so important
that what everyone says about us matters
We are filaments of dust, floating ash
Reacting in a dream world
Creating scenes
Fragments of reality
Delusional existence
Dissolved resistance
Figments
Elements
Imagination
Forgetting our hearts truest desire,
illumination

Golden

You are a plum in an orchard
attached to the tree trying to run free
When you fall, the cold grass nestles
Skin is your vessel until you shoot roots and become a tree too
You are built by grace and there is nothing left
but to surrender to this holy place
When you renounce your purpose
some may say you are running away
but only spirit determines your destiny
With your heart free, lend your love that is the seed
You are the love that can't be explained,
the heart that cannot be tamed
If you don't like where you are mentally,
renounce it and go within
Find the bow pulling your heart string
Radiate the song of love from where you begin
Only from this place can you dissolve everything

Growing Acceptance

Love is the only language God speaks
Everything else humanity made up, concepts
We are conceptualised
Judgement, sins, it's all lies
We are reflections of grace, living in a sacred place
Till we speak the tongue of God
there will be right, wrong and fears song
Know through your heart there is a bright arrow
opening you to what's always been true
That your mother tongue, is the language of God too
It is love from which you emerge,
and love to which you shall return

Mother Tongue

Put your seatbelt on
Buckle up at night before you take flight
Ready for lift off
Hold your soul in
You don't know where you begin
or where you'll wakeup
Have a lovely flight, sleep tight
Desire shapes our waking life
But we are not even here
Every night the 'I' likes to disappear
On planet Earth we think we are getting stuff done
But has the adventure even begun?
Could it be there is more than what we see?
Nothing in this world is concrete
We live on wings of the mind
We jump from idea to idea, fear to form
Without a clue of the essence of me and you
I fight for survival in feeling, breathing
I am a failed human
But what am I?
From where do I come?
Let's search the emptiness,
the light behind the shadows of night

Awakened Slumber

The world is an apparition
The mind the ultimate magician

Drift

~ Floating through space. Carried on wings.

Stars spring from the ends of her hair
Her aura is a rainbow
She walks on water
She blames herself for suppressing her truth
and speaking too loud,
for loving you
and killing her heart too
Pulling away from the swell, the place where fear likes to dwell
Swishing her tail and diving beneath the sea,
she has the soul of a selkie
walking on land
trying to understand man
When you break her heart, the whole world falls apart
But she'll sort through the pieces,
rebuild the fragments and from the ashes,
the universe is reborn

Wonderment

At the doors of truth, we leave behind intellect and mind.

Renounce everything you want to be
Let go of your imagined destiny
The glory and pain you think you may gain
Surrender to spirits plan
it will be better that anything you can imagine
Let go of trying to be your own description,
wipe clear the depiction
You are so harsh upon yourself
Surrender to the cards you've been dealt
Watch the fear of others melt
You are made of the fabric of time
Pull out of the picture
Become the lover of all
Whilst you secretly believe you are part of the painted scene
let God's touch guide your dream
You thought you needed a defined purpose
Bubbles of love are rising to the surface

Intuitive Joy

"Bury your feet into the earth, and grow tall and strong like me.
It's time for you to heal," said the wise old tree.
Filled with anger, you rang but you rejected me
I felt I was not enough for thee
so I place my head against the tree
who made my mind soft as water
The liquid that leads to light, a branch reaching for full height,
desperate for more sunlight
And though my jaw is still tight, my mind does not stir
The weight has left my back
I have the glorious tree to thank for that
I always knew we'd be friends
As I looked upon the tree from my window it's golden leaves
waved,
we connected
A soul who loves me even as others think
I've twisted round the bend
All trees grow their own way
Maybe you are a conifer and I'm a twig
I can be thankful I'm growing from a happy sprig
We turned back taking the same track
"Goodbye. Nobody has ever acknowledged me," said the beautiful tree.
And I cannot help but wonder why I was ever so sad,
at least you thought to call me
The winds may change but my roots still grow
and just like the tree I know I'm in the right place
Feeling love and all the while being blessed by divine grace

Out Walking

When they say your life has fallen into disarray,
sit on the mat and meditate
They don't want you to create a passage to freedom
to feel good
loved
safe
to live in a happy place
Expecting you to act like a machine,
living out someone else dream
You're a mess, if you don't pass our domination test
Allow the breath to rest
What if you were devoid of thought?
Desire?
Slipping between clouds escape the shadows trap
of
can
can't
won't
don't
Love is your treasure
It's freedom beyond measure

Secret Pathways

You have been chosen by God to spread words light and love
You are the peace keepers of this world

I crave the peace of God
in every breath I take, in every step I make
I pray you're being taken care of
I pray to wake up from this pain
for fear to dissolve,
for life to unfold
For me to trust in spirit is a must
I feel so angry that I feel scared
Why has spirit left me unprepared?
You tell me I am cared for
Spirit, take my fear, it's you who I want to be near
To let go, become hollow
Realise I am nothing and feel safe
immersed in the soup of holy grace

Invitation

The desire outweighs the fear
if you really want to do something.
That's how you find your path.

We wrestle with hunger and fight with shame
We make our hearts bleed again and again
We cut our throats
We bury our spirit
And yet we stand on solid land
Figures of existence, fighting acceptance with resistance
Hunting our hurts
Hiding self-worth
Witness the suffering
Watch the hollowness
Breathe deep into the dirt
Just let it be...
breathe
From the desert your soul emerges
Heat, stinging sand, your aura expands
Gently the dance begins
as your fears are drowned in the whipping wind
Twirl with love
Sink into grace
Let the beat of your consciousness caress your face
Fate dances the finale
On your last breath you'll breathe deep
to discover the beat of the heart never did rest

A cluster of candles lines a box, dull and motionless like rocks
A cluster of humans, shut their front door for one night more
We sit still
We embrace freewill and yet we all seem dead
By a spark, a candle is lit we feel our awareness shift
We feel the glow
The flickering flame burns low
Then it's our turn, our heart starts to burn
We discover the beauty of existence
and wonder why we ever resisted
The flame wavers
Soon it will disappear
as shall we,
forever
together
free

Light Me

You are already dead this world only lives inside your head
Recorded elements, filaments and flakes of fear
whispering in your ear
Particles of light, floating in the atmosphere
Twinkling stars making you feel you appear
You don't exist
You are nothing but bliss
Stripped bare you discover the 'you' is not even there
A remembrance of love projected into the ether
Existence fragile as a feather
floating wings
spiritual things
Air is what makes the bird fly
Discover your simplicity
You are the sky

Floating

You are the happiness that dwells within me
You are compassion in all beings
You are the love I'm seeing
Embrace the unknown only love is growing
Known, unknown, neither exists, only the mind persists
Release mental insults, it's not your fault
You are the child of love, a being of grace
In this moment you sit in a holy place
I bow to you
You know what to do
nothing, presence, grace
You emerge from the ocean of divine love
ruling your kingdom
of freedom, compassion and bliss,
a holy city where nothings amiss

My Everything

Healing, kneeling before your grace
thank God you took me to a holy place
For years I believed I would burn
I'd already sunk into the fires love, singed
Then I discovered that there is an end to pain
I let the fire take me, recreate me
I emerge from ashes, escape heated lashes
And here I stand, not human, not man
but an angel of God's plan
No matter how far you sink let yourself catch fire
Spirits kiss will take you higher
It doesn't matter what they say or who tries to get in your way
When you are the fire, you set everyone alight
Align them to love, their birthright
So thank your sins, your shortcomings
Knowing they are setting you free, from all you need to be
And as your mind is filled with pain
the only thing that can heal is spirits flame
Licking you up, your mind erupts from suffering and desire
a love fuelled fire
You light with simplicity
You've become the spark that dissolves the dark
And this is why the world needs you
to light those who suffer in grief,
to bring relief
I bow to your feet as you burn us all
and once more we fall
Illuminated in light we shift our plight
sinking into the heart, enmeshed in the spark

Wand

The pain in your heart is where healing starts

Divinity

~ That which is ever-present, never ending and all pervading.

My longing is only for us to unite again
You bait my breath with tenderness
You caress my body with grace
You make me lose sight of this place
I bow at Your feet
To You I admit defeat
I dedicate my life to surrender
You've planted the seed of wonder
This body has no roots
This spirit no seed
It's Your breath I breathe
I AM
Discovering where I began
Take all of me
I give my life to You
Take me over
Make me over
Spread your wings through my arms
Seduce me with your charms
I trust in the majesty of presence,
Your immortal essence

Fill Me

You are inspirational because you exist
Your presence is a gift to the world

You are a seed of light and to feel happy is your birthright

Your beauty doesn't sleep
You are not skin deep
You transcend time and sit wide awake to meet your prince,
but he doesn't exist
You don't lay in a tower
You've already claimed your power
You rule your own kingdom, inner dominion
Undaunted by thoughts, negative taunts
you sit in wisdom
Immersed in light your kingdom shines bright
You are the ruler of you, living in luminosity
You shower the world with generosity
A princess who doesn't need a throne
A queen with no king
You really are something
A sight to behold
Living in a palace of gold
You give your jewels away
Armies come from afar
to throw their weapons to the floor
With love you greet
and the world is laid before your feet

Sacred Royalty

The moon still shines it's light upon me as it slips behind trees
I bath in its luminosity
Full and bright, I am pulled towards its might
Wondering, could walk upon its shine
that ripples across the sea?
I am so desperate to be free, to escape reality,
to be someone other than me
I long to follow its golden glow into its beams I want to go
The path that leads up to the stars
Some think I'm crazy
My mind is hazy
I'm drunk on liquid light, ready to take flight
into the golden shimmer, so I can disappear
A sun, I rise each morning
I am a piece of this place another luminescent planet
created by God's grace and though I cannot see
there are a million things that depend on me
and this doesn't make life hard for that is part of spirits facade
It's just that I've forgotten my place
as a creation of God's majesty
So I let go and watch your glow
It pulls to the surface my life's purpose
that although I am nothing
I am part of something
I bow to your light
I am pulled to clear the suffering that's hidden in my mind

I realise I am a rock swirling in God's solar system
I have found my place
Like you, I am a swirling ball of grace

Moonlight Magic

Dissolve into the atmosphere let yourself disappear
There is no sky
There is no me
There is no you
because there never was two
There is no self
Drink from the fountain of wealth
One day you will grow out of what you believe
and then you shall feel relief
In life we witness through a keyhole
our perspective wide as a peephole
Open your vision
Melt division
One day your life will be gone
All the world is a lie
Ignore the mind
Do not comply to distraction, reaction
Heal in nothing
Break free from the illusion that you are something
Discover who you are, follow the 'I' to the source
Truth is found in silence
Quieten mind violence
Start at the start
Dissolve in the heart

Invisible

Searching in silence you crave the eternal lovers light,
the kiss of spirit, a love affair
Desiring happiness you wonder,
maybe you should stay a little longer?
But time is now my friend
Spirit lives through you
You are happiness itself, this is true

They're blissing out when you're about laughing in madness
Feel the gladness
When half the world is popping pills
so they don't have to feel, just to stay present,
you sit there covered in glee
Illusion dissolved in simplicity
Your energy is wonderful
Light of laughter, white light bliss that we're all after
The energy so high we're touching the sky
and everyone is heaven baked
whilst we sit here wide awake

Joy in Presence

Looking for love we seek grace from above
We desire perfection, haunted by our greatest deception
~ that we are unlovable
We all want to be liked, want to do what's right
Definitions of good are dominated, dictated
Quivering we decide we hate what is us
and this is what breaks us
If you could only see your soul
your perception would shift of how your life's story is told
You glitter in gold
You are heaven scent
You are the breath of empowerment
You are the love for the person who appears off track
You are grace
You are majestic
You are the light in the heart
You are the peace behind the fear, the grace behind the black
You are forgiveness of doubt
You are blames mother's love
You are everything and nothing
And when you surrender to you,
you dissolve the idea of two
and become the compassion in all beings
the love, we are all needing
seeking
being

In Your Grace

Division of light and sound creates a path into the void
No longer escaping the you, you'd rather avoid
Take the lift to pure consciousness
Transcend into bliss
Twirling on a staircase of stars
Devote all to surrender
Let your heart remember

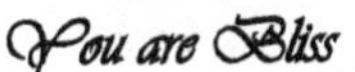

There is no free will
There is no individual
We are brainwashed to think we are we
that I am she and he is he
You are nothing but divine awareness, the awakened one,
whose light shines bright as a thousand suns
Even those who think they're separate, bereft,
they are nothing but blank screens living in a dream
You are the screen
You are no-thing
It's why you feel worthless, lost without a purpose
But you arise from the nothing
Only your ego thinks you're something
Nothing isn't dead,
it isn't hatred,
it isn't anything
A love elixir, this is where you begin
All you are is angelic, beyond immortal relic
You are all that exists, a flash of consciousness
Don't think
Be free
Drop you
and realise you are not even peace
not even bliss
just a figment of divine consciousness

Live Well

There is beauty in every step
There is beauty in every breath
My life is sacred
Your life is sacred
The world is a pathway to the discovery of self
eternal love
oneness
infinite light

I am gone
I don't exist
My soul has faded
The carpet of humanity has been vacuumed
We are all projections of light illuminating from the heart
and when your light goes out you simply restart
remiss
relax
recover
You are an illusion of consciousness
a dream
a ripple of divine play
leela
Everything is becoming clearer
We don't paint our life, for there is no brush
We dissolve into atoms, universal substratum
Have compassion for all, they are you after all
And you are not even alone
You have vanished like smoke from whence you came
Surrender your mind to the divine game
It's not important and neither are you
for you are all that is spirit
and that is beyond importance
creation
salvation
imagination
No longer suppressing the light your soul takes flight
dipping and diving
forgetting striving
Doubt is the veil between you and God
Through eyes of innocence God will appear
For God is ever near
See beyond the cloud of doubt,

the concept you are somehow without
Place your eyes in your heart
and view the world with simplicity
God shall be the only thing you see
Have you got it?
For you will know
God is ever-present with only love to show
Feeling the breath of peace from which you emerge
the universal serge of love
Hands clasped in prayer
You awaken as you realise *love* is everywhere

The discovery of who you are
is the greatest gift you can give to the world
For as your mind and soul meet
your heart acquires a new beat
love resonates
infinite light radiates
Cloaked in robes and unusual clothes
we long to emulate the monk
To travel to afar, where incense twirls
and exotic spices entice our senses
Where mountains caress our back
and for just one second you can relax
Why not do it now?
Give yourself the power to take away expectation
See the spark already shining in you,
the sacred seed of stillness
that can be found on isolated plains,
mingling with the scent of summer rains
Or on a boat adrift at sea
with nothing but sapphire rippling waves far as the eye can see
Or a lofty island where no man lives and only the birds make
you feel you are somehow, tangibly linked to reality
Or right now in this very space
where holy silence blesses your grace
There is only this moment
Erase the words of this rhyme to lose your mind
You have everything to gain
Throw your pain away and love will settle in to stay
See there is no veil blinding you
No shores to visit, or mountains to climb
You are already divine

With Love

Love is what you are
The breath caught between my tender lips
My heart's warm beat
Chilly ocean waves caressing warm flesh
The stars alight reflecting a darkened night
The invisible thread of life
The grace that wraps fear making it disappear
Words from a sacred tale
The beauty of nature cradling us all
Pieces of you held together by thought
The light of your existence
The suns glow
The moons shadow
Love is what you are

You are in the right place
You are in the right time
You are supported by the divine
You are where you are
You've travelled so far so you could be here now
You were sent by spirit
Everything is perfectly in place, twirling in luminous space
The consciousness that manifested you
knows just what to do
You are here to discover the self, your sacred heart
Your soul floats in bliss
Your essence is peace consciousness
You are beauty itself in human form
You know where to go
There is no map for *that*
Sit still
feel the heart
acknowledge it's real
and fall back into grace
The place you were racing too
that has always,
forever,
lived within you

Remarkable

Your Path

There is no greater desire in life than to be loved. We are all looking for love. This book is titled, *I Still Love You* because I can't help but think of it as the one line that I personally would most like to hear. So I figured maybe that is what others would also like to hear and if it could brighten someone's day in the slightest possible way, well that would be wonderful.

We are here by the grace of God, Spirit, Consciousness that tangible sense of all pervading love, light and bliss. Something bigger than your mind has put you here, and this is what leads me to believe that there's something bigger to trust in than all of our minds. We are made of magic and stardust. Intrinsically we all are love. To love is our basic nature, it's our basic beingness. Love is what we are. Loving everything is simple, we are love. When we look deep within, past the 'I', past the you, me, he, she, we discover the radiant light of love in our heart. A love beyond human conditional love, the love that makes the planets sparkle, the Divine Love that beats our heart every second.

Most often we spend our lives looking for love, never realising that deep, glowing, ecstatic harmony we seek always comes from within. It is always felt through our being; we are not separate from it. We think love is something we have to acquire. Love is a reflection of the divine within you, when you feel love for something or someone, that love shines through your heart.

Our perception of how to get love is unique and different depending on our cultural conditioning. The way we were raised and the ways in which we perceived we received love when we were little. Or the way in which a lover lit our heart when before we felt scared and or unwanted. Love is flirtation with the self. Divine Love is seeing the sacred heart of bliss, peace, everlasting consciousness reflected in all beings.

Most often we look for love in lovers, in the mirror, in our bank accounts, in our parents' eyes. We look for love by saying yes, even when we mean no. Suppressing our soul truths in the effort to be loved. By beating ourselves up about not being good enough because we believe when we are good enough we will be lovable. Dis-identifying with our ego is the key to being able to see with eyes of love. When we transcend beyond our thoughts, we discover Divine Love is what we already are.

Love is honouring yourself and accepting where you are at right now. It's saying what you feel. It's hating yourself. It's trying to be better. It's making mistakes. It is the regret that taints our days. It's the lover that ran away. It's shame. It's the music in the trees. It's stars sparkling over the ocean. It's the pain, the hurt, the despair, in truth Divine Love is everywhere. It is the essence of your being, and as much as we deny its existence it is all-encompassing and present in each moment. In every second of every day, no matter how destructive or blissful we feel we're all being guided to discover the truth of our heart. It is found in the shadows and in light. Love is everywhere and all-encompassing.

The mind likes to distract from the truth of your being. From the truth found in the hearts of all beings and all life. It is a divine blessing that we can look beyond the mind to discover the formlessness and the consciousness from which we are made.

Humanities violence scars our perception. We are all traumatised as we blindly fight for our place in the collective. People are defensive, we fight for careers, for our rights, for our family, we fight against bullies, we fight to be seen as good - so that we may receive more love. And we are left feeling terrible and traumatised when we don't receive the perception of love we so desire. This need to fight and defend pulls us away from the moment. Fighting creates teams, it creates winners and losers, kings and queens, peasants and pickpockets.

Everyone wants to win and when someone feels like they are losing, self-esteem sinks and self-hate rises to the surface. But there are no winners. When that which made someone experience the feeling of winning - pride, ego, vanity - is stripped, a loser remains. We are all victims to the wheel of destiny. We may attract joy and we may attract suffering. Instead we need to practice non-reactance. Tuning to our heart and being guided by this grace rather than a desperation to 'be something'. True grace is found in the heart and from here a life of peace, compassion and wisdom is lived.

We are all human and we are having the experience of good, bad, right, wrong, success or failure. When we can accept where we are at and what is playing out in our life peace can be found. When we can witness the rotation of our emotions from love to hate, happy to sad, we make space for the grace we all crave. The stillness of Divine Love.

I trust in spirit to take my hand and lead me in the way universal consciousness has planned

You are in the right place. There is nothing wrong with you and there never will be. Anyone who tells you otherwise is trying to deconstruct the bright light that is you. They have lost connection to the light which shines bright within themselves and instead of desiring true awareness and they seek to escape pain in the folds of life. The feeling of being intrinsically flawed is something we all try to escape from. We try to meet the definition of perfection that is a projection.

The more we try to meet someone else's expectations the more we disconnect from our humanity. We allow our fears, and the dark night of the soul to cloak our being. We become less human and more inhumane. Your perceived flaws and mistakes are the essence that make you complete. They are the medicine to your healing.

We use drugs, food, self-sabotage, denial, pain and thought to suppress our being, our humanness, and this is tearing humanity apart. Sickness cloaks our soul in the feeling of being flawed. This idea that you cannot fail, or you will be shamed. This idea that it is wrong to feel; lonely, isolated, down, sad, dejected, worthless, rejected. These feelings are shadows and tears hovering about your persona, they are steps guiding you to reject what you've been taught and who you think you are. When you feel pain, you are holding the suffering of the world in your heart.

The more we recognise divinity and love in our own hearts, the more we accept grace as a valid option for humanity. Don't back out, or back down from your fears, your inner hatred. They are there painting your soul with colours of fear and guilt, and from this grows seeds of light. This world is a dualistic space and dark and light intermingle. It's realising that as low as you may feel there is always light. That you were born for a reason. That you have power and courage within you.

I feel like we shrink from our existence, not because we are so bedridden in self-loathing (though it can feel like this) but because we are so terrified of what we would do if we honoured our soul. And deeper still if we were honouring our soul would we still be flawed - unlovable?

When you discover the truth of who you are love is

unveiled. Compassion and kindness rule your destiny. You are nothing but love. In the karmic wheel of life many people have forgotten the truth of their essence. Seek who you really are, beyond your minds labels. Beyond what you've been told defines you. You are goodness. You are beloved. You are grace. You are kindness. You are a gift of God. A divine expression of light, compassion and love.

If you've ever felt like taking your life and checking out, you are not alone. There are so many brave souls who are so disgusted with themselves and disenchanted with the planet that these beautiful light beings are escaping into the wilderness of eternity. But you are here now and you are reading this message, and I know it's because you are a light warrior, a being of eternal bliss. If you weren't here on this planet, you would be missed. Your presence is helping everyone who feels stuck, to question their reality. Your presence, is waking people up.

For a minute don't think of the horrors that weigh so heavily upon your chest. What you've done or haven't done. Who loves you and who doesn't want you. Think of what you'd like to change in the world. Think of homeless families, children trapped in paedophile rings, refugees, starving people, orphanages overflowing with children, innocent animals being slaughtered. Think of what really sparks fire in your chest, those things that don't benefit you, but are destructive to all beings. The things in our world that pull souls down to the ground in terror: rape, poverty, famine, war, armies of destruction.

If you really want to die, maybe you could instead stand up, and speak up, speak about what breaks your heart. Speak for the wellbeing of others and all creatures, love and the unity of humanity. Speak of kindness, self-respect, and the right to find your own path. For people to be able to make mistakes and heal. Put yourself on the firing line where so many others are too scared to stand. If you really want to escape, you may as well go out with courage where so many others are too scared for their lives to do so.

Terrifying right? The idea of being loud in a dictated, shame, blame, and guilt ridden world is pretty frightening. But we need you. We need you here, to link arms, to see beyond racism, religion and beliefs and to shine the light of love. The light hidden in your heart, that has always been there and always will be shining so, so brightly. You are you. You are worthy. You exist because you are a gift from the divine.

Thank you for your voice. For your courage. For your ability to honour your soul. You don't have to do what anyone else says or does. Just listen to your heart. It knows the way to honour your soul and how to bring you back from the brink of death. From the brink of self-hatred and fear of the unknown. After all, how did you arise into this planet? Is what you see real? Are your emotions telling you the truth?

Depression is waking up. Suffering is waking up.
Love and compassion is living.

I can't wait to meet you and see the light you bring and already are.

Namaste

Peace. Peace. Peace.

Poetry Index

U

V

W

Y

About the Poet

Nerissa Marie, shares light and love throughout the universe. She sends blessings and smiles to all who surround her. Nerissa Marie is an author, naturopath, and mystic. She believes all beings are equal, sacred manifestations of the divine and that when we recognise the divinity within all beings, including ourselves, we create a pathway to inner-peace and a harmonious planet.

Life is a journey and all emotions and experiences; pain, despair, failure, success, joy, happiness are healing tools guiding us deeper within ourselves, until we discover the source of our true being, bliss and love. She looks forward to meeting you on the journey to sacred union and to the awakening of humanity as all hearts unite in infinite peace.

Her goal is to serve universal spirit, and realise eternal love. A few of Nerissa Marie's favourite things include crystals, meditation, fairies and raspberry vegan smoothies. She has an immense amount of gratitude, to be living on planet earth and for the intertwining of her reader's spirits, on the dance of life, as she shares her heart through the written word.

Namaste.

NerissaMarie.com

Inspirational Books by Nerissa Marie

Available on Amazon and most other retailers in Hardcover, Paperback, Kindle and Epub format.

Peace, Love and You is a self-help, spiritual guidebook that empowers you to look at the true nature of your being; divine love, compassion, and bliss. You are perfect, whole and complete simply because you exist. You are a divine expression of love. Peace, Love and You is an inspirational book that aims to empower your soul with inner wisdom.

When fate hands you the perfect woman, it's easy to know what to do. For Hugo de La Laville, life's a little more complicated. He has three perfect, potential fiancées…
Paris Mafia Princess, explores the time we waste on trying to get even and finding the right partner at all costs. How our natural competitive instinct can be used constructively, and why we sometimes forget that the most important relationship we have in life is the one we develop within ourself.

Abyss of Bliss, is an inspirational poetry collection exploring the purpose of life. Pain, guilt, regret, shame and lack often haunt our life. This spellbinding poetry book, goes beyond emotion, beyond form, beyond belief and explores the resounding truth of peace, love and wellbeing hidden in the heart. A beautiful collection of soul healing love poems that reach into the depths of the soul.
We are nothing more than beams of light floating through consciousness. Projecting desires in the abyss. All the while forgetting we are pure, simple, humble manifestations of bliss.

FREE GIFTS! Future releases, free book promotions, and more!

Available at **NerissaMarie.com**

All is well, you were never born and you will never die, for your true nature is the spirit of love consciousness, bliss playing in eternity. You will always be loved as your essence is that. Be still, be silent …Awaken

CPSIA information can be obtained
at www.ICGtesting.com
Printed in the USA
LVHW051554020123
736269LV00019B/547